OUR GOVERNMENT

THE U.S. HOUSE OF REPRESENTATIVES

BY ELLA CANE

CAPSTONE PRESS
a capstone imprint

First Facts are published by Capstone Press,
1710 Roe Crest Drive, North Mankato, Minnesota 56003
www.capstonepub.com

Library of Congress Cataloging-in-Publication Data
Cane, Ella.
The U.S. House of Representatives / by Ella Cane.
pages cm. — (First facts. Our government)
Includes bibliographical references and index.
Summary: "Informative, engaging text and vivid photos introduce readers to the U.S. House
of Representatives"— Provided by publisher.
ISBN 978-1-4765-4201-0 (library binding)
ISBN 978-1-4765-5145-6 (paperback)
ISBN 978-1-4765-5998-8 (ebook PDF)
1. United States. Congress. House—Juvenile literature. 2. Legislators—United States—Juvenile
literature. 3. Legislation—United States—Juvenile literature. I. Title.
JK1319.C28 2014
328.73'072—dc23   2013032202

Editorial Credits
Shelly Lyons, editor; Kyle Grenz, designer; Wanda Winch, media researcher;
Eric Manske, production specialist

Photo Credits
Corbis: Jose Luis Magana, 15; Courtesy of the White House: Pete Souza, 9, Lawrence Jackson,
1; Getty Images: AFP/Saul Loeb, 5, Alex Wong, 11, Bill Clark, 13, Bloomberg/Pete Marovich,
cover (middle), Chip Somodevilla, 21, CQ Roll/Tom Williams, 19; Newscom: CNP/Ron Sachs,
17; Shutterstock: Anatoly Tiplyashin, cover (star, stripes design), Mesut Dogan, cover (Capitol
building); U.S. House of Representatives, cover (logo)

Printed in the United States of America in North Mankato, Minnesota.
092013   007771CGS14

TABLE OF CONTENTS

CHAPTER 1
Making the Rules 4

CHAPTER 2
Branches of the U.S. Government 6

CHAPTER 3
A Bill Becomes Law 8

CHAPTER 4
Who Can Be a Representative? 10

CHAPTER 5
Serving Many People 12

CHAPTER 6
A Representative's Job 14

CHAPTER 7
A Representative's Day 18

CHAPTER 8
The Speaker of the House 20

Glossary 22
Read More 23
Internet Sites 23
Index 24
Critical Thinking Using the Common Core 24

MAKING THE RULES

Have you ever wished you could make the rules? You could if you were in the U.S. House of Representatives!

The U.S. House of Representatives is in the legislative branch of the U.S. government. Members of the legislative branch make laws for the nation.

IN GOD WE TRUST

CHAPTER 2

BRANCHES OF THE U.S. GOVERNMENT

The U.S. government has three parts. The executive branch makes sure laws are being followed. The judicial branch explains the U.S. **Constitution** and makes decisions on laws.

In the legislative branch, the House of Representatives and the Senate make up **Congress**. Together they work in the Capitol building in Washington, D.C.

Constitution—the written system of laws in the United States; it states the rights of people and the powers of government

Congress—the elected group of people who make laws for the United States; it includes the House of Representatives and the Senate

8

FEDERAL GOVERNMENT

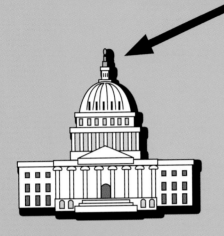

The U.S. Capitol

LEGISLATIVE

CONGRESS

SENATE

HOUSE OF
REPRESENTATIVES

The White House

EXECUTIVE

PRESIDENT

VICE
PRESIDENT

The Supreme Court

JUDICIAL

SUPREME
COURT

7

CHAPTER 3

A BILL BECOMES LAW

Ideas for new laws can come from the president, Congress, or other people. From these ideas, members of Congress write **bills**. **Representatives** present and **debate** the bills, and then they vote. If a bill passes in both the House and the Senate, it goes to the president. The president signs or **vetoes** the bill. If he signs it, the bill becomes law.

bill—a written idea for a new law
representative—a person elected to serve the government; U.S. representatives serve in the House
debate—to discuss between two sides with different ways of thinking on a subject; each side tries to convince people that it is right
veto—the power of the president to keep a bill from being approved

FACT House members write and study thousands of bills each year. But only about 4 percent of the bills become laws.

CHAPTER 4

WHO CAN BE A REPRESENTATIVE?

There are rules about who can be a representative. Representatives need to be U.S. **citizens** for seven years or more. They must be at least 25 years old. They must also live in the state where they are **elected**. Once elected, representatives serve a two-year **term.** They can run for office as often as they like.

citizen—a member of a country or state who has the right to live there
elect—to choose someone as a leader by voting
term—a set period of time

FACT Congress meets from January to late fall. Members of Congress live in Washington, D.C., during that time.

CHAPTER 5

SERVING MANY PEOPLE

People in every state elect leaders to serve in the House of Representatives. The House has 435 members. States with many people have more representatives. For example, California has 53 representatives, but Vermont has only one. Each representative works for the people of his or her home state.

The first House of Representatives met in 1789. There were 65 members.

CHAPTER 6

A REPRESENTATIVE'S JOB

Representatives have many duties. They meet with people to talk about ways to make the country better. They study ideas and suggest bills. Representatives also help set up **taxes** and decide how tax money should be spent.

tax—money that people or businesses must give to the government to pay for what the government does

Each representative also serves on two committees. A committee focuses on a certain area, such as **agriculture**. Representatives also run their own offices. Each representative has a **staff** and a **budget** to keep track of.

agriculture—the science of growing crops
staff—a group of people who work for the same company or organization
budget—a plan for spending and saving money

CHAPTER 7

A REPRESENTATIVE'S DAY

Representatives often attend meetings. Some days they meet in small committee groups to talk about bills. Other days they meet in a large group to vote on bills. Representatives may also go to events at the Capitol. They meet with other government leaders. They also visit with people from their home states.

CHAPTER 8

THE SPEAKER OF THE HOUSE

The Speaker of the House is the leader of the U.S. House of Representatives. Representatives elect the Speaker. During large meetings the Speaker asks members to talk about bills. The Speaker also meets with the president and leaders of the Senate to talk about bills.

FACT When a new Congress begins, representatives vote to elect the Speaker of the House.

Amazing but True!

The Speaker of the House often bangs a wooden gavel on a desk. The Speaker uses the gavel to begin and end meetings and keep order. The gavel is also used to signal when it's time to vote. The gavel sometimes breaks from so much use. In fact, gavel heads have even flown off handles into the House seats.

GLOSSARY

agriculture (AG-ruh-kul-tuhr)—the science of growing crops

bill (BIL)—a written idea for a new law

budget (BUH-juht)—a plan for spending and saving money

citizen (SIT-i-zuhn)—a member of a country or state who has a right to live there

Congress (KON-gress)—the elected group of people who make laws for the United States; it includes the House of Representatives and the Senate

Constitution (kahn-stuh-TOO-shun)—the written system of laws in the United States; it states the rights of people and the power of government

debate (duh-BATE)—to discuss between two sides with different ways of thinking on a subject; each side tries to convince people that it is right

elect (i-LEKT)—to choose someone as leader by voting

representative (rep-ri-ZEN-tuh-tiv)—a person elected to serve the government; U.S. representatives serve in the House

staff (STAF)—a group of people who work for the same company or organization

tax (TAKS)—money that people or businesses must give to the government to pay for what the government does

term (TUHRM)—a set period of time

veto (VEE-toh)—the power of the president to keep a bill from being approved

READ MORE

Harris, Nancy. *What's the State Legislative Branch?* First Guide to Government. Chicago: Heinemann Library, 2008.

Nelson, Robin, and Sandy Donovan. *The Congress: A Look at the Legislative Branch.* How Does Government Work? Minneapolis: Lerner Publications, 2012.

Shea, Therese. *Meet the House of Representatives.* A Guide to Your Government. New York: Gareth Stevens Pub., 2013.

INTERNET SITES

FactHound offers a safe, fun way to find Internet sites related to this book. All of the sites on FactHound have been researched by our staff.

Here's all you do:

Visit *www.facthound.com*

Type in this code: 9781476542010

Check out projects, games and lots more at
www.capstonekids.com

INDEX

bills, 8, 9, 14, 18, 20
branches of the U.S.
   government, 4, 6

Capitol building, 6
committees, 16, 18
Congress, 6, 8, 11, 13

first Congress, 13

number of
   representatives, 12

president, 8, 20

representative's duties, 8,
   9, 14, 16, 18
rules about running
   for the House of
   Representatives, 10

taxes, 14
terms, 10

vetoes, 8
voting, 18, 20, 21

CRITICAL THINKING USING THE COMMON CORE

1. States with many people have more representatives. Do you think that's a good policy? Say why. (Key Ideas and Details)
2. Representatives write bills. If you were a representative, what bill would you like to become law? How would you go about getting support for it? (Integration of Knowledge and Ideas)